Tomorrow Is Near
But
Today Is Here

Asaf Rozanes

To my Mia
the passion, light and power behind everything I do

Welcome one and all, let's meet our new friend.
Her name is Mia, and she'll be with us till the end.
She smiles, she grins, and like you, she is kind.
She thinks about things with a positive mind.

Yet let's start from the beginning,
When things were not this.
Instead of thinking she worried,
and what a day she would miss!

When Mia worried about stuff,
Time passed by in a zip.
Kids playing, friends laughing,
And she missed a field trip.

As Mia worried about stuff,
She missed out on new things.
Like playing new games,
Or even what magic can bring.

As Mia worried about stuff,
Time began to disappear.
She missed an entire spring day,
Like she was not even here.

Butterflies flew around her,
A lion escaped from the zoo.
Wild monkeys danced with canes,
And there was a unicorn too!

Although she was "there" just under the tree.
She was distracted by worry, which she could not even see.
A cloud was shaped like a rocket, there were three bears that walked by.
A man walked on a tightrope, and someone ate a whole pie.

When she looked all around,
She could see the day was now lost.
She walked home feeling sad.
Worrying came at a cost.

That's what happens when you worry about things that could change.
We miss all the wonderful things, even things that are strange.

If you want to change something, just think about it this way.
Why worry about it now, when you can just do it today!

Our time is precious you see,
We only get so much in a day.
So why waste it with worry,
When you can read, paint, or play.

Mia missed all of those things,
And she felt so sad in the end.
She did not play or have fun,
Or even have time with friends.

When she got ready for bed, she was still worried and sad.

Until her father came in, and could see she felt bad.

He leaned over and told her a marvelous thing.

How to think about the good, and what tomorrow might bring.

"Today may be over,
Yesterday is too late.
Yet tomorrow will come,
And you can make that day great!"

"Keep your eyes open.
Keep your smile real wide.
Keep your heart happy.
And leave no worry inside."

"Don't worry about the bad things.
Instead *focus* on the good.
Don't stress about what you don't know.
Just *Think* about what you should."

"Now Mia listen to me, when you start to worry and scare.
Just take in a deep breath, and let it out into the air."

"Enjoy your time today,
Enjoy your time right now.
Everything will work out,
The way it's meant to somehow."

"Today creates tomorrow,
So, do the most that you can do.
Yesterday has passed,
and tomorrow is something new."

"Instead of worrying lots, just smile real wide.
Focus on today and you'll be happy inside."
He kissed Mia goodnight, and she curled up in her bed.

She took a deep breath, and thought of good things instead.
Mia practiced right then, and thought of happiness too.
And what do you know! What Dad said was true.

So that is the story of Miss Mia you see,
Who knows how to smile, and think happily.
She smiles, she grins, and like you, she is kind.
And now we all know how to keep a positive mind.

Mia and Dad sprinkled and scattered love all over this book!

Were you able to notice and find all the heart shapes we scattered around?

Spoiler Alert:

The next page contains all the hidden locations, flip the page at your own risk ☺

Pssst…Here's where we hid the heart shapes:

<u>Page 5:</u>
On the curb, beneath Mia and the dog
On "Grandma's" pink dress

<u>Page 9:</u>
On the calendar above the bed
On Mia's umbrella

<u>Page 11:</u>
On the clouds in the bottom right part of the page

<u>Page 13:</u>
Beneath the left column beside the house door

<u>Page 15:</u>
On the top left part of the red curtain

<u>Page 17:</u>
On the purple ball

<u>Page 23:</u>
On the carpet

<u>Page 25:</u>
On the lion's mane
On the left side clouds

If you liked our book and want to help us write many more – please take a minute and write us a review on Amazon;

Reviews help our books get noticed and other kids and parents to experience and enjoy our creations.

Thank you!

Join "Mia and Dad" on their journeys in these books as well:

- Short or tall doesn't matter at all
- Part of the rainbow
- The Monster Friend

and many more to come…

Want to be the first to hear about our new books and special offers?

Subscribe to our private mailing list here:

https://mindful-mia.com/subscribe

Mia and Dad just LOVE to color and we're sure you do too!

So we've added a few of our early book sketches just for you to color in any way you like.

Make the sky pink and the grass blue, it's all up to you!

Printed in Great Britain
by Amazon